For SKIPPER

Horses & Riding

By J. K. Anderson

Author of
*Horsemanship
in Ancient Greece*, etc.

Drawings by
Nancy Conkle
Cover by Donna Neary

From the Tournament
Book of Duke William
of Bavaria, 1529: *Bayer-
ische Staatsbibliothek*

Bellerophon, left, was, according to the best authorities, the inventor of horse-manship. The goddess Athena gave him a magic bridle with which he caught and tamed Pegasus, the winged horse who sprang from the neck of Medusa the Gorgon when her head was cut off by Perseus. Pegasus used to come down every evening to drink at the fountain which had sprung from the print where his hoof first touched the earth, and here Bellerophon lay in wait for him.

Mounted on his winged steed, the hero entered Corinth. The Queen of the city fell in love with him, but he virtuously rejected her. She told her husband the King that Bellerophon had tried to seduce her, and the King sent Bellerophon to his friend the King of Lycia in Asia with a sealed letter, which contained a demand that the bearer should be put to death.

The King of Lycia was afraid to attack Bellerophon, so set him three dangerous tasks, of which the greatest was to kill the fire-breathing Chimaera—part lion, part goat and part serpent. Bellerophon succeeded in all of them, with Pegasus' help, and so won the hand of the King's daughter, and became King of Lycia after him.

From a cup by Euphronios, c. 510 B.C.   *Antiken Sammlungen*, Munich

Xenophon of Athens, the friend and pupil of Socrates, is the author of the oldest book on riding that has come down to us, though we know that he had several centuries of experience to draw upon. Much of his basic advice on buying your horse, stable management, schooling and riding is still useful today. "Remember that a beautiful horse with bad feet is no more use than a beautiful house with bad foundations." "Horses don't understand speech, but learn to associate conventional noises

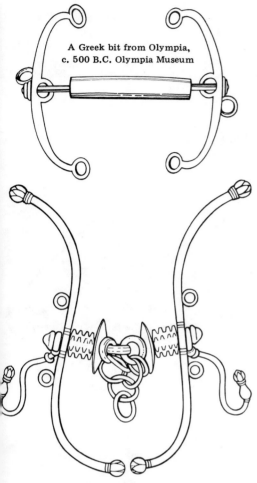

A Greek bit from Olympia,
c. 500 B.C. Olympia Museum

A Greek bit from Boeotia, c. 350 B.C.
Staatliche Museen, Berlin

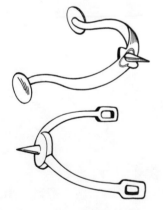

Greek spurs from Dodona, 300 B.C.
Dodona Museum

with particular behavior; reward them when they do well and punish them when they displease you, and they will soon understand." "Calm your spirited horse by long slow rides, not by galloping him to a standstill." "Above all, never lose your temper when dealing with horses or with children."

Xenophon had been a famous soldier as a young man, though his book was written in his old age—perhaps about 365 B.C.—"for our younger friends." His advice is often intended to prepare horse and rider for cavalry service. War games and competitions in sports like throwing the javelin from horseback are good training; hunting on horseback is still better, if suitable country and game are available, which perhaps they seldom were in Greece. Jumping, up and down banks, over walls and thorny barriers round sheepfolds, is necessary for a horseman who has to ride across country fast and safely, but Xenophon does not regard it as a spectacular and exciting sport; safety first, and hang on to your horse's mane to avoid jobbing his mouth.

Xenophon was probably not a racing man, but races, both for chariots and ridden horses, were among the most popular events at the Olympic Games and other big sporting festivals. They were always on the flat - a furlong's straight gallop, round a pillar making a hairpin turn, straight back again, and repeat for as many laps as the event called for. The spectators were accommodated on earth banks or wooden bleachers on each side of the narrow track, and spills were common, especially at the turns, but did not always bring disqualification. We know the name of one mare, Aura, who finished the Olympic race without her rider but was given first prize, perhaps more for the perfect manners with which she stopped after passing the post than merely because she had arrived first.

Greek horses were small, with fine heads but rather coarse bodies. The Greeks rode bareback, or at best on saddlecloths, and used very severe bits, with spiked rollers and sharp-edged disks round the mouthpiece. (Xenophon says that you should also have a smooth bit, so that when the horse has been schooled with the help of the severe mouthpiece you can ride it on the mild one.) The *psalion,* a metal noseband or cavesson, was also sometimes used. This pressed on the outside of the nose when the reins were pulled, and prevented the horse from throwing up his head to escape the action of the bit.

From a vase by the Sisyphus Painter, c. 420 B.C. *Antiken Sammlungen,* Munich

Castor's horse, from a vase painting by Exekias, c. 530 B.C. Vatican Museum

The Greeks perhaps invented spurs, which were a novelty in Xenophon's time, though soon afterwards they were a recognized part of the horseman's dress. Young show-offs used to swagger about the market-place in spurs to show that they belonged to the cavalry.

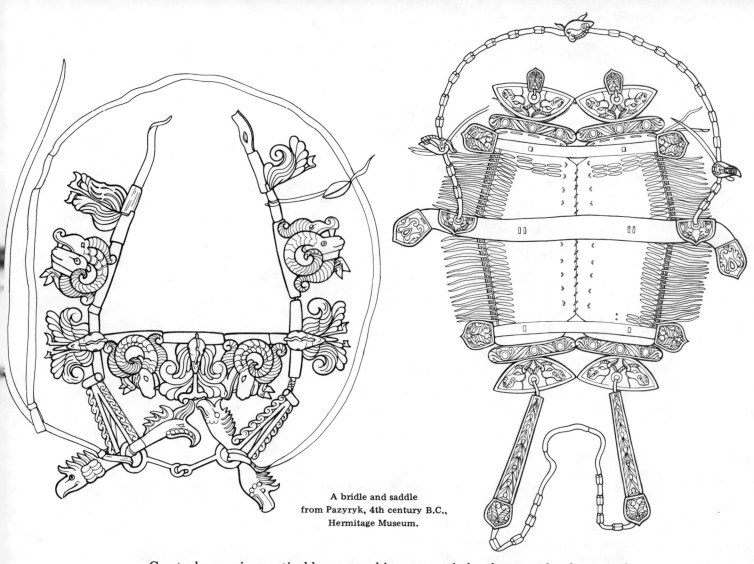

A bridle and saddle
from Pazyryk, 4th century B.C.,
Hermitage Museum.

Great advances in practical horsemanship were made by the nomads who ranged on horseback from the Ukrainian steppes across Central Asia as far as China, but did not know how to write and so have left us no handbooks. The Scythians, at the western end of this range, were well known to the Greeks. A silver vase made by a Greek artist about 350 B.C. shows a Scythian hobbling a saddled pony. Far to the

Detail from Chertomlyk
Amphora, c. 400 B.C.
Hermitage Museum

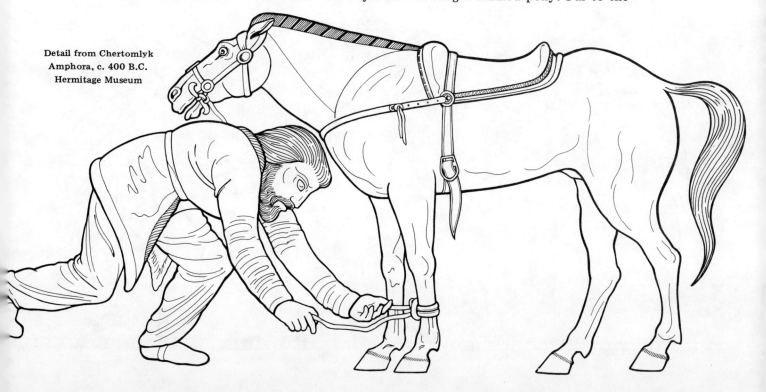

Hermitage Museum

east, at Pazyryk in the Altai Mountains of Central Asia, burials of chieftains with their horses and gear have been preserved by permanent frost and we can follow the rapid development of the saddle, from the narrow cushions, one on each side of the horse's spine, connected by wooden arches front and back, (about 400 B.C.) to saddles, with regular trees (less than a hundred years later).

    None of these saddles have stirrups, but the extra security that they gave the rider may be one reason why the Pazyryk horsemen could manage with comparatively mild bits. Their bridles were elaborately decorated with carved and gilded wooden ornaments. They had no buckles, and so knotted and stitched the leather straps ingeniously. Notice that the off-side rein slips through a loop in the end of the near-side rein, so that it can be used to lead the horse or tie him up.

From a comb from Solokha, c. 400 B.C. Hermitage Museum

The nomads developed a riding dress suited to a life on horseback in a climate of extremes—cap with ear-flaps to guard against frostbite; heavy, long-sleeved jacket; long trousers tied into ankle-length boots (without heels: heels originally came in with the stirrup to stop the foot from slipping through). They were constantly at war, over cattle and grazing rights, and their weapons and tactics also fitted their way of life—a powerful bow, short enough to be used on horseback, carried on the left hip in a case that also served as quiver; a light shield of wicker that could be managed together with the reins; sometimes a battle-axe: a short sword, in a heavily-ornamented sheath which was tied down to the right thigh like the holster of a cowboy's six-shooter, and ended in a metal chape, to stop the point from working through and running into the thigh as the rider swung his leg over his horse's back in mounting. (The wicked King of Persia Cambyses was killed in this way—stabbed by his own sword in the very place where he had himself wounded Apis, the sacred bull of Egypt.)

In some of the nomad tribes the women rode herd, and even into battle, with the men. Sometimes girls were not allowed to marry until they had killed an enemy, and, if they never did, they died as old maids. When the Greeks met these warrior women, north of the Black Sea, they decided that they must be descended from the Amazons, who had fought against Hercules, Theseus and Achilles. To explain how they had found their way from the heart of Asia Minor, where the old legends placed them, they made up a story about how three shiploads were being carried back to Greece as prisoners, but overpowered their guards, and drifted to the north of the Black Sea. After landing, they seized a herd of grazing animals, and made a living

From a Siberian gold plaque, 4th - 3rd century B.C., from the collection of Peter the Great, Hermitage Museum, Leningrad

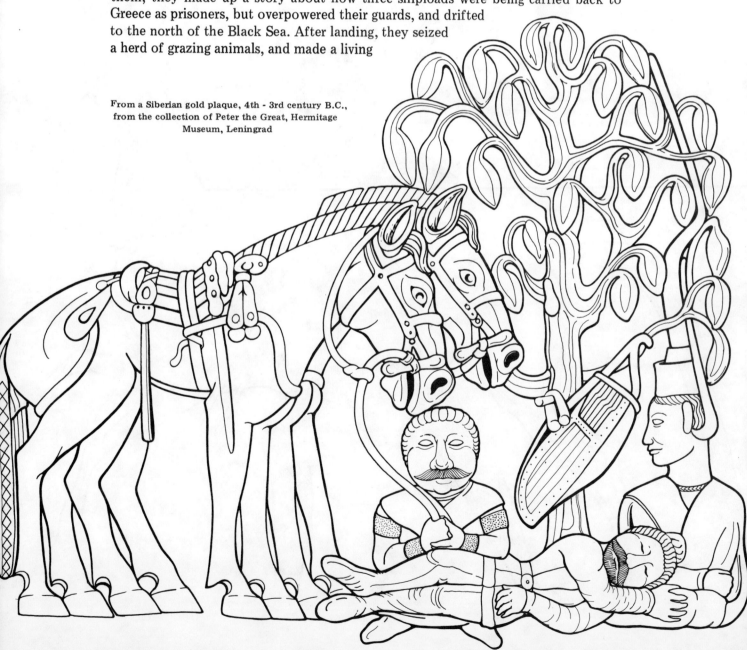

hunting and raiding the Scythians. The Scythians at first gave battle, but found from the bodies of the slain that the enemy were women, and resolved to save this noble breed and unite it with their own. So they told some of their own bachelors to shadow the Amazons, without fighting them. Soon one of the young men met a girl who had become separated from the others; they fell in love; introduced others of their friends; and before long marriages had been arranged for the whole of both groups. But the Amazons would not go and live with their new mothers-in-law, who led a relatively sheltered existence in covered wagons, and insisted on migrating eastward with their husbands to found a new tribe.

The Greeks also changed their old stories, to make the Amazons, who before this had been imagined as foot-soldiers armed mostly in the Greek fashion, into horsewomen, and horsewomen they have remained ever since. At first artists painted them in nomad costume; later Greek tunics were thought more becoming than jackets and trousers. But they kept their horses as well as the battle-axe and the crescent-shaped shield. In fact, whenever the Greeks and the Romans after them

An Amazon from an *oenochoe* by the
Mannheim Painter, 450 B.C.
Metropolitan Museum
of Art

came across these shields they thought that the Amazons could not be far off. So the story grew up that when Alexander the Great was fighting the nomads in Central Asia the Queen of the Amazons sought his hand in marriage, and much later Roman soldiers who found these shields on a battlefield in Asia thought that they had defeated the Amazons and were disappointed to find that all the prisoners were men.

A seated Amazon, above, and below foiling an attacker, from a Roman sarcophagus c. 150 A.D. Capitoline Museum, Rome

A Roman auxiliary cavalryman,
from a relief in the
Mainz Museum

The Romans, whose splendid infantry conquered the world, were not outstanding horsemen. Their best cavalry came from the peoples they had conquered—the Numidians of North Africa, who rode bareback and without bridles, but had taught the Romans a sharp lesson when Hannibal led them into Italy; and the Gauls, Julius Caesar's old enemies. The Gauls possibly share with the Greeks the credit for inventing the spur. They seem also to have invented the curb bit, in a very severe form, in which the horse's jaw was held between a mouthpiece as savage as the worst Greek ones and a metal rod or bar passing beneath the chin. Long cheekpieces, to the ends of which the reins were attached, gave the rider the advantage of a levering action.

The Gauls also used plain ring snaffles, very like the ones still used today, but cast from bronze and beautifully enamelled. These were probably for driving, not riding. Some of the Gauls went on using war-chariots until the third century B.C. and their British cousins were still using them when the Emperor Claudius landed in Britain in A.D. 43.

From the Gundestrup Cauldron, Copenhagen

The Gauls used fully developed saddles, with high pommels and cantles, which probably provided the model for the type later used by the Roman Imperial Cavalry. Like the nomads, they wore trousers—when we talk of "riding breeches" today we are using the Gallic word "bracae."

Another Gaulish invention is the horseshoe, which was certainly in use in the Alpine region in the first century B.C. and in the Pyrenees not much after. But cavalry chargers and other ridden horses do not seem to have been shod—only draught animals, including mules, and pack-ponies in mines, and on the new Roman metalled roads.

Hipposandals—detachable metal shoes which could be fastened over injured feet to allow them to recover—were used by Roman farriers and veterinary surgeons.

From the funerary monument of the Julii, Saint Remy, Provence; 1st century B.C.

To most Romans, equestrian sports meant the chariot races, which attracted huge crowds to the circus—a racecourse shaped like the old Greek ones, but built up artificially. The races were elaborately organized with teams—originally Red, White, Blue and Green representing the Four Seasons; later Blue and Green only, paid for by the Imperial Government, and employing professional drivers, who, like modern professional athletes, became the idols of the mob. Big-game hunting on horseback and mounted combats were also popular spectator sports in the Arena. The performers were again professionals, or sometimes prisoners of war.

Roman aristocrats, who provided the officers for the cavalry regiments, kept horses, and hunted. The Emperor himself usually set the example.

The poet Martial cautions a friend, in about 90 A.D.—

Dear Priscus, don't ride on that hard-pulling mare,
Or gallop so fast in pursuit of the hare.
Too often the hunter turns victim, and lies
Where he fell off his horse, never more to arise.
Though you still skirt the hedge and the ditch and the wall,
The plain's hidden perils may give you a fall.
You'll see lots of riders come off, every Meet.
Let's hope they are lucky and land on their feet!
If you must have blood-sports, take a tip from a friend,
The more dangerous game brings less risk in the end.
Let's go and hunt boar; with your galloping habits
You'll come to more grief than you bring to the rabbits.

Boar hunting was very dangerous if you faced the charging beast with a spear in your hands. But there was no need to take more risk than you wanted to. Pliny the Younger describes how, when he had to appear for appearance's sake at the hunt, he brought a good book with him to kill time while he waited by the nets into which the boars were driven.

Most Roman women never rode. But there were exceptions like Caesonia, the favorite of the mad Emperor Caligula, who scandalized society by appearing on horseback at reviews of the guards: Martial's friend Juvenal was shocked by fast girls, dressed like charioteers, whose admirers took them out driving on the main roads in broad daylight. Ovid advises the lover to take his girl to the races:

Crowded together in the Stand
You needn't merely touch her hand
But can rub shoulders where you sit
And - make *her* choice *your* favorite.

Above: from a silver dish from Pompeii, National Museum, Naples; below: from a mosaic from Thysdrus, Bardo Museum, Tunisia

The Little Hunt, from a mosaic in the Piazza Armerina, Sicily; c. 300 A.D.

Perhaps for some Romans the Hunt Breakfast, with the horses safely tied up, cushions laid out under a neatly-rigged awning, and the servants bringing a good supply of wicker-covered wine bottles, was the best part of the day.

Queen Dido of Carthage, whose tragic story was told by Virgil, was a famous legendary huntress. Here she rides to the hunt with her false lover Aeneas, watched by the god Pan, ruler of "the mountain-goats who bound

From rock to rock, and keep the craggy ground."

Dido and Aeneas after Poussin, c. 1654; Prado, Madrid

A Persian king hunting, from a silver plate in
the Bastan Museum, Tehran; 4th century A.D.

For nearly four hundred years the Persians threatened the frontiers of Rome, and of the Eastern Empire which survived when Rome itself fell to the Goths. In the end, both Empires were worn out, and in the seventh century A.D. both were defeated by the Arabs, inspired by the teaching of Mahommed and mounted on the hardy mares of their native deserts. "Aim at their eyes! " the Arab leader called to lightly-armed lancers as they charged the mail-clad Persians.

An Arab Prince hunting, c. 750 A.D., from a
hunting lodge in the Trans-Jordan Desert

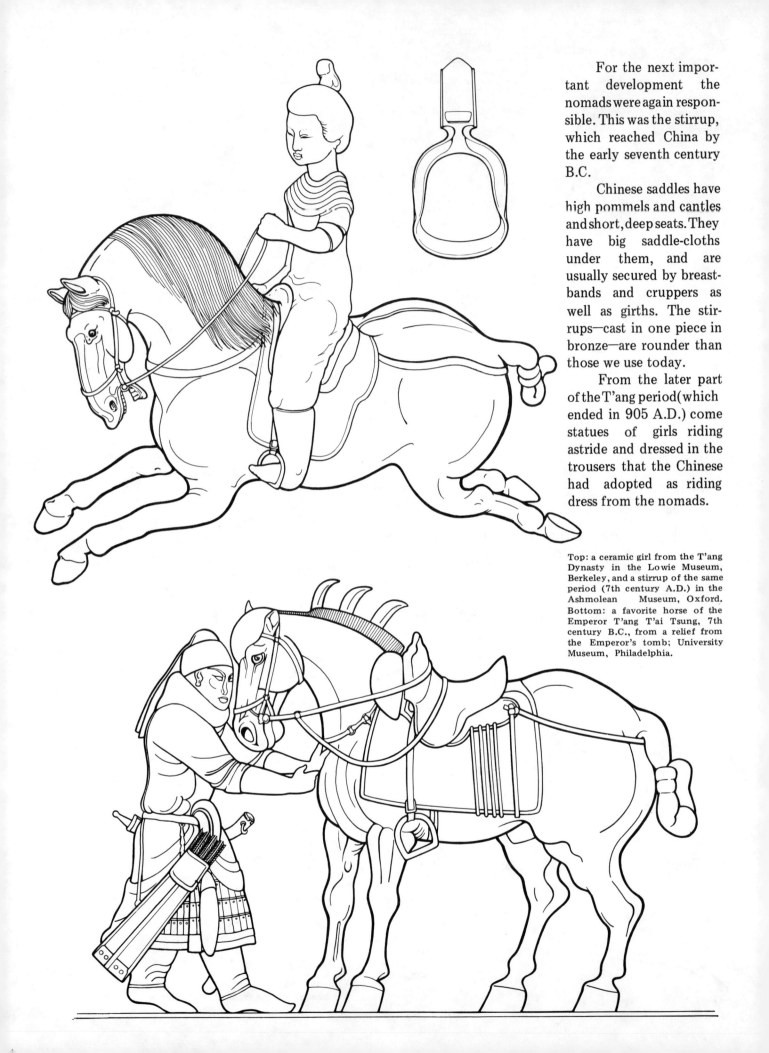

For the next important development the nomads were again responsible. This was the stirrup, which reached China by the early seventh century B.C.

Chinese saddles have high pommels and cantles and short, deep seats. They have big saddle-cloths under them, and are usually secured by breast-bands and cruppers as well as girths. The stirrups—cast in one piece in bronze—are rounder than those we use today.

From the later part of the T'ang period (which ended in 905 A.D.) come statues of girls riding astride and dressed in the trousers that the Chinese had adopted as riding dress from the nomads.

Top: a ceramic girl from the T'ang Dynasty in the Lowie Museum, Berkeley, and a stirrup of the same period (7th century A.D.) in the Ashmolean Museum, Oxford. Bottom: a favorite horse of the Emperor T'ang T'ai Tsung, 7th century B.C., from a relief from the Emperor's tomb; University Museum, Philadelphia.

From the St. Ambrose Altarpiece, Milan Cathedral; prior to 835 A.D.

In Western Europe, the Franks and Norsemen were probably using stirrups by the eighth century A.D. (Saint Ambrosius of Milan nearly loses his, in a picture dating from 835 A.D., as his horse shies at a heavenly vision.)

Western cavalry develops a different style of riding from the Easterners, with the stirrups very long. The rider's legs are almost straight: perhaps it was hard to bend them in heavy mail.

The Bayeux Tapestry shows the Normans riding against the Saxons in this style at Hastings in 1066 A.D.

Norman knights hurrying to Hastings, 1066; from the Bayeux Tapestry

The Crusades, which began in 1096 A.D., matched the chivalry of Western Christendom against Turks and Saracens who were lightly armored, used javelins or bows on horseback, and rode in the Eastern manner with short stirrups and a balanced seat. The Christian knights used heavy lances, tightly clamped between the upper right arm and the body, so that the whole weight of horse and rider were behind the lance. Their saddles had very high pommels, to protect them in front, and high cantles, to save them from being carried over their horses' croups by the shock of impact. They rode with their legs straight and stiff, braced against the stirrups.

Top: from Queen Mary's Psalter, c. 1320; bottom: from the Luttrell Psalter, c. 1340; British Museum

The first meaning of "chivalry" was "horsemanship." The knight's gilded spurs were a practical part of his equipment as well as a status symbol. As armor developed, with plate being added to chain-mail in the fourteenth century and replacing it altogether in the fifteenth, spurs became longer—not just for show but because long spurs were needed if the armored rider, on an armored horse, with his thighs almost enclosed in a massive saddle, was to reach his horse's sides. Since long prick spurs could do serious damage, rowels were invented, which also made the spur more decorative.

Above and right, from the Manessa Manuscript, c. 1275; *Universitaatsbibliothek*, Heidelberg

A firm seat, the courage and ability to ride his horse straight at the enemy, and the skill needed to pull him up short after the charge and turn him round again, using an ever-more-elaborate and powerful curb bit, were the essentials of knightly horsemanship, both in the battlefield and in the tournament. In a tournament in 1390, "the Earl of Huntingdon sent his squire to touch the war-target of the Lord of Saimpi. They couched their lances and pointed them at each other. At the onset their horses crossed, not withstanding which they met. But by their crossing, which was blamed, the Earl was unhelmed. He returned to his people who rehelmed him: and having resumed their lances they met full gallop and hit each other with such force in the middle of their shields that they would have been unhorsed had they not kept tight seats by the pressure of their legs against the horses's sides...The Earl grasped his spear again, and the Lord of Saimpi, seeing him advance at a gallop did not decline meeting, but spurred his horse on instantly. They gave blows on their helmets, which were luckily of well-tempered steel, which made sparks of fire fly from them. At this course the Lord of Saimpi lost his helmet but the knights continued their career and returned to their places. This tilt was much praised."

Given a fair field, the knight could hope to carry all before him. But faced with obstacles he was at a disadvantage. We hear of one knight who jumped a stone wall into a vegetable garden during a skirmish, but could not get out again, and after blundering about for some time had to surrender to the old woman whose cabbages he had spoiled. And sometimes whole armies of knights met spectacular disaster when they tried to charge steady infantry posted behind obstacles. In the church of

From *Le Coeur d'Amour*
of King René; 15th century

Courtrai were kept hundreds of gilded spurs stripped from the French knights who had been killed by Flemish burghers in 1302. At Crécy in 1346, and at Poitiers ten years later, the English archers wounded and terrified the French horses, so that they became uncontrollable and threw their riders. And the English knights themselves had been defeated in 1314 by the Scottish spearmen who drove them back among the marshes of Bannockburn.

From *Le Coeur d'Amour*
of King René, 15th century

In the Middle Ages horses provided the only alternative to walking for those who wished to travel by land. Heavy covered wagons could convey passengers where roads—usually the remains of the Roman road system—permitted. But riding was faster and more comfortable, for both men and women. Chaucer's Canterbury Pilgrims show that not only the knightly class but lawyers, merchants, sailors and scholars could ride—though no doubt the Clerk of Oxenford was happier on a horse as lean as a rake, than he would have been on a spirited animal. The Wife of Bath, who had

"On her feet a paire of spores sharp"
probably rode astride, though she wore
"A foot-mantel about her hipes large."

The Prioress and her nun no doubt rode sidesaddle, as did the ladies who went a-Maying with the Duke of Berry on their fat palfreys a few years later. The farmer's wife going to the market, or the court lady on a country outing, might prefer to ride pillion, seated sideways on a comfortable thick pad behind a man who of course rode astride on a normal saddle.

From Queen Mary's Psalter, c. 1320; British Museum

From the *Très Riches Heures du Duc de Berry*, 1410; Chantilly, *Musée Condé*

The mediaeval sidesaddle had neither stirrups nor a pommel over which the rider could crook her knee. She sat sideways as though on a bench, with both feet supported by a horizontal footboard. She would have found trotting extremely uncomfortable, so her palfrey was bred and trained to amble. And of course she could not have ridden across country.

But in old books there were pictures of girls hunting, "winding the horn, rousing the game, and pursuing it, without any other assistance. They ride astride."

Once a horsewoman was safely in the saddle, she could arrange her dress becomingly, but mounting presented a problem. A Burgundian knight describes Maria, the Empress of Constantinople (who rode astride, unlike Burgundian ladies of the time) taking horse to ride home after a dinner-party:

"They brought her a bench, on which she climbed. Then they led up to her a very fine trotting horse saddled with a beautiful rich saddle. Then one of the ancient noblemen who attended her took hold of a long mantle which she wore and went to the other side of her horse and stretched out the mantle on his hands as high as he was able. She set foot in the stirrup, and mounted on horseback in just the same way as a man. Then he threw the mantle over her shoulders and gave her one of those long pointed Greek hats, on which, along the point, were three golden plumes, which suited her very well. She seemed to me as beautiful as before" (when he had seen her in church) "or even more so. She came so close to me, that they told me to step back, and it seemed to me that one could find no fault in her, except that she painted her face. There certainly was no need, for she was young and fair." The ladies in waiting, "who were also very beautiful and dressed in mantles and hats,"mounted in the same way as the Empress, and the party rode off to the palace of Blachernae.

From Good Government in the *Palazzo Publico*,
Siena, by Ambroggio Lorenzetti; 1337-9.

Bertrandon de la Broquière, the Empress's admirer, had found the Turkish saddles, on which he rode all the way from the Holy Land to Hungary, very uncomfortable to begin with. He was used to the European seat, with long stirrups, and after sitting all day as though in a chair, in a deep saddle with high pommel and cantle, short stirrup-leathers and large stirrups, he was so stiff that after dismounting he needed help to remount.

But in Spain, where Christians and Moors had been in close contact for centuries, it was the mark of a true cavalier to "ride in either saddle." Horses went with the Spaniards to the New World almost as soon as it was discovered, and both styles of riding went too. When Cortes landed in Mexico in 1509 his horses helped even more than steel and gunpowder in the conquest of the great Aztec empire by a handful of adventurers. "After God, we owed the victory to the horses," says Bernal Dias, who had served under Cortes and in his old age set down from memory an account of the Conquest. He remembered the horses as well as he remembered his human comrades, and describes each one individually. The Indians at first thought that horse and rider formed a single terrifying monster, and were still afraid even after they realized that they were dealing with men mounted on animals. In fact, on at least one occasion when the two "halves" of one "monster" parted company accidentally they were more frightened than ever.

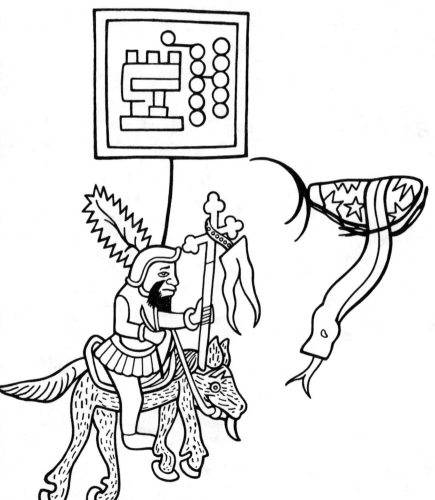

But the Lady Marina, an Aztec princess who was converted to Christianity, learned to ride, and accompanied Cortes as guide and interpreter on his long march through Central America in 1525.

On this march, Cortes's own black horse hurt his foot, and had to be left behind with a tribe of Indians who promised to look after him. But sacrifices of chickens and offerings of flowers failed to save him: the horse died, though no Spaniard returned that way to learn his fate for nearly two hundred years. Then in 1697 missionaries found the tribe still worshipping a statue of the horse, which they had set up in their chief temple.

Nuñez de Guzman goes to Jalisco, from the *Codex Telleriano Remensis*, 1529

The Emperor Charles V, leading his armies to victory over the Protestant League at Mühlberg in 1547, provides an excellent example of the straight-legged European seat. He is in half-armor; cavalry equipment was being made lighter as it was found that armor was ineffective against cannonballs anyway.

The Emperor Charles V after Titian, c. 1548; Prado, Madrid

Other horses that were abandoned or lost by the Spaniards proved more fortunate. During the two centuries after the Conquest, great herds of wild horses bred from strayed animals, especially on the grasslands of the North American Prairie and the South American Pampas. Indian tribes soon learned to capture and ride horses, and some completely changed their way of life. From being settled forest dwellers, they took to a wandering existence on the Great Plains, following the vast herds of buffalo, which they could now hunt on horseback, and fighting wars which were aimed largely at stampeding and running off the enemy's horses. They used lances, and bows and arrows. For shooting on horseback, many of them found, as the Asiatic nomads had done before them, that the balanced seat with short stirrups was best.

As the descendants of the Spaniards and other European settlers coming from the Eastern seaboard advanced across the plains, and cattle replaced the buffalo, the military saddle of Western Europe, which was descended from the saddle of the knights, was further developed to suit the work of the cowboys. The skirts of the saddle were enlarged, so as to spread the rider's weight over as much of the horse's back as possible. The pommel was strengthened, to become the roping horn. Wooden stirrups replaced the metal ones. And the deep seat, with the rider's weight slightly back, his legs straight, and his feet braced in the stirrups, was as secure on a half-wild buckjumper as it had been in the lists.

After Catlin, c. 1840

"The Bolter" after C. M. Russell, 1904

Meanwhile in Europe a new sort of cavalry had developed. Instead of a lance, the trooper now carried, in holsters fastened to his saddle, two huge horse-pistols, each nearly a yard long. Cavalry were drawn up several ranks deep, and would halt a few yards away. The front rank would fire their pistols, then retire to the rear to reload while the second rank took their place and so on. All this called for great control.

One of the last commanders to use cavalry in the old knightly fashion was the Duc de Joyeuse. In 1587 he led the French King's men-at-arms against the rebellious Protestants, who were armed with pistols in the new style. The long line of knights broke under fire and the Duke, in his golden armor, found himself alone and surrounded by his enemies. "I am the Duke, and my ransom is ten thousand crowns! " he shouted. But someone put a pistol ball through his head.

How much happier are huntsmen than soldiers! "In stead of Pystolets, they shall have each of them a bottle full of good wyne at the pommell of their saddles."
—Turberville's *Booke of Hunting*

All the gentlemen in Europe were flocking to Italy to acquire the learning of the Renaissance—classical literature, fencing with the newfangled rapier and poniard instead of the good old English sword and buckler, the use of forks instead of fingers when dining in polite company, and of course the art of riding the Great Horse. Federico Grisone of Naples published in 1550 the first textbook of horsemanship since Xenophon's and it has been claimed that his Academy represents a revival of classical Greek horsemanship—part of the general rebirth of Greek learning. But, unlike Xenophon, he was more concerned with showing the horse who was master than with helping it to understand what its rider wanted. He used deep-seated saddles, long spurs and long-shanked curb bits, inherited from the mediaeval tradition, and advised his readers to break in young horses by putting them into a pit and beating them about the head. If later on the horse refused to go forward when he was mounted, some of Grisone's followers had the answer—tie a hedgehog under his tail, or let a footman stand behind you with a savage cat fastened to a pole, and push it between the horse's hind legs. Of course, these remedies might lead to "the contrary vice of running away."

After Cuyp, 1650; Royal Collection

Horse, Pistol and Cavalry Soldier; a 17th Century Cuirassier

Riding the Great Horse was not of course for women. But a new style of side-saddle riding had also been brought from Italy—according to tradition by Catherine de' Medici, who married the future Henry II of France in 1533. Instead of merely sitting sideways on a sort of padded armchair, with both legs side by side and both feet supported by a horizontal board, the horsewoman now crooked her right knee round the pommel of the saddle and used a stirrup for her left foot. The man's saddle was changed to a sidesaddle by moving the pommel slightly to the left and adding a fork to give extra support for the right leg. The horsewoman could now sit with her body facing the front, and had enough grip to be secure at the trot, canter or gallop. She would not need to jump very often, as the countryside, both in Britain and on the Continent, was still open, with unenclosed fields. (Men did not often jump obstacles either: at least textbooks say almost nothing about the subject).

Queen Elizabeth I of England used to ride to hounds, telling her courtiers that the young should follow and the old might stay behind. She herself kept up the sport until the end of her life. "Her Majesty," says a courtier writing to Sir Robert Sidney, "is well and excellently disposed to hunting, for every second day she is on horseback and continues the sport long." At this time Her Majesty had just entered the sixty-seventh year of her age.

Queen Elizabeth I's saddle, from Turberville's *Booke of Hunting*, 1576

Queen Henrietta Maria, from an engraving c. 1640

But not everybody approved, especially of girls who went further than the Royal example justified them in doing. An author of the seventeenth century speaks of another fashion..."The Bury ladies that used hawking and hunting were once in great vein of wearing breeches, which it seems give rise to many severe and ludicrous sarcasms. The only argument in favor of this habit was decency in case of an accident. But it was observed that such accidents ought to be prevented in a manner more consistent with the delicacy of the sex, that is, by refraining from these dangerous recreations."

From Antoine de Pluvinel, *Le Maneige Royal*, 1626

It soon became clear that it was better to gain the horse's confidence and cooperation than to force him to do what he did not understand. Antoine de Pluvinel studied in Naples when he was young and when he was old became the teacher of King Louis XIII of France. His book, published after he died in 1620, has on its title page pictures of Science, who leads her winged horse with the greatest of ease though her nose is buried in her book, and Force, whose spiked bludgeon cannot control his unruly animal. "Horses cannot obey or understand unless we caress them constantly, by voice, hand or the present of sugar or some other titbit when they behave, and punish them promptly when they misbehave...Be sparing with punishments and generous with rewards."

Pluvinel's book is in the form of conversations between himself and his royal master. He starts with the right clothes to wear (if His Majesty has any doubts, here is the Duke of Bellegarde, Grand Esquire of France, dressed just as a gentleman ought to be). His Majesty will notice the difference between a "fine" horseman and a "good" horseman: he himself cannot fail to become both, and never has Pluvinel seen poor old Bonité go so well for any other rider than His Majesty! After mastering the High School airs, His Majesty goes on to martial exercises, and finally tilting.

In the reigns of earlier kings, men-at-arms had trained in time of peace by trying to carry away at the lance's point a ring hung just at the height of a horseman's eye. They rode in full armor, but now that lance is no longer used in war, cavaliers wear their ordinary dress, (ram your hat down so that it won't come off!). This is "so that the ladies can honor the riders...For when the competition is over the cavaliers can enter the carriages of the most beautiful (with their permission) without keeping them waiting... When a newly-wed bride or another lady has given a ring so that the cavaliers may compete for the love of her, the one who gains it wins much honor and great joy."

That is all that Pluvinel has to say about horsewomen.

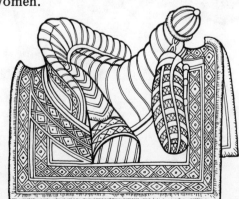

Pluvinel: saddle & *chambrière* -foot assistant's whip

About the same time as Pluvinel, Gervase Markham, an Englishman, wrote a handbook of "Cheape and Good Husbandry for the Well-Ordering of all Beasts and Fowles," and tells his reader how to "make a perfect horse in three moneths, fit either for pleasure or battell." Markham does not write for kings and courtiers—"Our English Gentry...aim for the most part at no more skill than the riding of a ridden and perfect horse, which is but only the setting forth of another man's vertue...Yet our English Husbandman or good-man, whom I seeke to make exact and perfect in all things, shall not only recreate himself in riding the horse whom other men have made perfect, but shall by his own practice bring his horse from utter ignorance to the best skill that can be desired in his motions."

The Husbandman, unlike the King ("We will not even speak of such beasts in front of Your Majesty" says Pluvinel) is interested in all sorts of horses besides the Great Horse "for a Prince's seat." Travel, hunting, racing, light and heavy draught and pack-horses are all mentioned. "Turk" and "Barbary" horses were already being crossed with native English breeds, laying the foundation for the stock from which the Thoroughbred was to develop in the next century.

The Husbandman will need "a good and easie travelling horse" for his "occupation in the generall affaires of the Common-wealth, as some to the markets, some to the City, and some to the seates of justice." He must know how to condition his hunter, bringing it in from grass "about Bartholemew Tide (September), the day being faire, dry and pleasant." But his best profit will lie in making and selling Great Horses, trained not only in strictly military movements but in "other salts and leaps,

The Duke of Newcastle's horse, from *La Méthode Nouvelle et Invention Extraordinaire de Dresser les Chevaux*, 1658

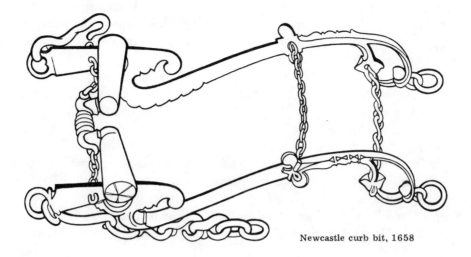

Newcastle curb bit, 1658

right pleasant and curious to behold, and though not generally used in the wars not utterly uselesse for the same.''

Markham's system is based on helping the horse to understand what is wanted of him by means of Helps (as we say nowadays aids), Cherishings (when he obeys the aids) and Corrections (when he does wrong)...When the young horse makes even a small move in the right direction "cherish him a little, and so to the lessons again, which if he doth orderly or disorderly yet cherish him exceedingly, that he may come to the true knowledge of your meaning." Corrections might be given through the bit, the spur, the whip and the voice "delivered sharply and roughly, as ' Ha villain! Carridro! Diablo!' ''

From the Duke of Newcastle, 1658

In 1642 the sons of the "Gentlemen" and "Husbandmen" for whom Markham had written his book took up arms "for King or for the Commonweal" in the civil war between King Charles I and his Parliament. Prince Rupert, the King's nephew who led his cavalry, was an excellent pistol shot (he once got into trouble for picking a weathercock off a church spire) but there were not enough pistols to go round: most of his men came to war mounted on hunters, with their grandfathers' swords by their sides. So cavalry again charged home to fight hand to hand, and at first the King's Cavaliers usually swept the Parliament's troops off the battlefield—"gentlemen's sons, younger sons and persons of quality" fighting against "old decayed serving-men and tapsters, and such kind of fellows." But when Oliver Cromwell organized his "Ironsides"—"sober, God-fearing men" under "plain russet captains," who charged at "a round trot" and so stayed under control instead of galloping off in headlong pursuit—the "gentlemen's sons" were beaten in their turn. The Marquis of Newcastle, the King's General in the North, fled to the Continent, and since his huge fortune had been confiscated by the Parliament, made his living by conducting a riding academy at Antwerp.

Newcastle wrote a book (in French: translated into English in 1743) describing his "New Method of Dressing Horses," in which he criticizes "some people, who as soon as they have got upon a young horse...fancy that by beating and spurring they will make him a dress'd horse in one morning only. I would fain ask such stupid people, whether, by beating a boy, they could teach him to read, without first showing him his alphabet." Newcastle is even more scornful of the philosophers who deny that the horse can think. When "the clouds darken, though the horse knows not these words, *dark, cloud, lightening, thunder*, both he and I will not withstanding take to our heels to shelter ourselves from the rain under the trees...It is true, that the horse cannot express his reasoning by a proposition...whence he has at least this advantage, that he never errs as men do...What makes scholasticks degrade horses so much proceeds (I believe) from nothing else but the small knowledge they have of them, and from a persuasion that they themselves know everything." Newcastle reminds his reader that "if a man has lost his way in a dark winter's night, let him leave the horse to himself and the horse will find the way," and ends his remarks on philosophers by saying that "a scholar and a horse are very troublesome to one another, and so I leave them without giving them or myself any further trouble."

His own method (like Xenophon's) was based on "the hope of reward and the fear of punishment;" beginning with "the True Seat and the necessary Actions of a good Horseman" and "the Movements of a Horse in all his natural Paces" he proceeds to "How to Dress a Horse in all sorts of AIRS" and finally to "all the Vices belonging to Horses and the surest way to cure them."

His illustrations have as their background his lost mansions and estates. In one of them a stag hunt is going on in "le Parc de Welbeck." But Monseigneur le Marquis is not interested: he and his horse are performing Courbettes in solitary splendor, with their backs turned to the hunt.

And though a girl, mounted sidesaddle in a long habit and a picture hat, forms part of a hawking party outside the Castle of Ogle in Northumberland, the Marquis pays no attention to her either. The ladies make no other appearance in his book, except as admiring spectators.

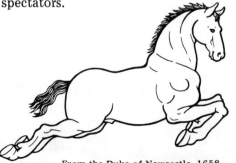

From the Duke of Newcastle, 1658

In 1660, after Cromwell was dead, King Charles II "enjoyed his own again." But times had changed: the deer-parks of the nobility had gone under the plough; open fields and commons were being enclosed with hedges and ditches. So the country squire gave up the heavy military saddle in which he had ridden to Worcester fight, put a flat saddle on his horse's back, shortened his stirrups a few holes, and turned to fox-hunting instead of the more formal and expensive stag-hunt. His daughters learned to "gallop all day after a fox and all night after a fiddle"—not just in the country but at Court too. They still rode sidesaddle, but gradually adopted more practical clothes. On June 12th 1666 Samuel Pepys went to the King's palace at Whitehall and found "the Ladies of Honour dressed in their riding garbs, with coats and doublets with deep skirts, just for all the world like men...with perriwigs and with hats; so that only for a long petticoat dragging under their men's coats, nobody could take them for women in any point whatever."

The Duke of Newcastle, from his *General System of Horsemanship*, 1743

Fifty years later, in George I's time, Alexander Pope described in a letter how he "met the Prince of Wales with all his ladies on horseback coming from hunting... We all agreed that the life of a Maid of Honour was of all things the most miserable and wish'd that every woman who envy'd it, had a specimen of it. To eat Westphalia ham in a morning, ride over hedges and ditches on borrowed hacks, come home in the heat of the day with a fever, and (what is worse a hundred times) with a red mark in the forehead from an uneasy hat; all this may qualify them to make excellent wives for fox hunters, and bear abundance of ruddy complexioned children."

But here is a description of Lady Henrietta Cavendish-Holles-Harley (Newcastle's granddaughter) hunting her own pack near Cambridge—

On fair *palfrey* well equipt did sit
An Amazonian dame; a scarlet vest
For active horsemanship adaptly fit
Inclos'd her dainty limbs; a plumed crest
Wav'd o'er her head; obedient by her side
Her friends and servants rode; with artful hand
Full well she knew the steed to turn and guide;
The willing steed receiv'd her soft command.

Lady Henrietta Harley after Wootton,
1726, Welbeck Abbey.

Here is another eighteenth-century description of hunting girls:

How melts my beating heart as I behold
Each lovely nymph, our island's boast and pride,
Push on the generous steed, that sweeps along
O'er rough, o'er smooth, nor heeds the steepy hill
Nor falters in the extended vale below

Somerville, *The Chace*

After Thomas Rowlandson, *The Chase*, 1790; Courtauld Institute, London

Meanwhile the crack riders of England (and of North America, where fox-hunting in the English style did not end with the War of Independence) rode across country in a style that seems very unscientific nowadays. The "top sawyer," "sitting well back, getting his horse by the head, and giving him a refresher with the whip," despised the "craners" who were always peering over the hedges to see what was on the other side before risking a jump, no less than the "circus tricks" of the European academies.

These great men went the pace in every way, outside the hunting-field as well as in it. Squire Mytton was once driving a gig with a nervous passenger, who said he had never been in an accident, did not want to be in one, and begged the Squire to slow down. "What?" said Mytton. "Never been upset in a gig? What a dull fellow you must be!" and promptly ran one wheel of the vehicle up a steep bank so that the whole thing tipped over onto the road.

Hunt dinners were formidable affairs. "The M.F.H. will bring his night-cap with him, for where the M.F.H. dines he sleeps, and where the M.F.H. sleeps he breakfasts."

Top Sawyers, after John Leech, 1854

About the middle of the nineteenth century the sidesaddle was improved by the addition of a "leaping head," a sort of horn that curls over the rider's left thigh and prevents her from being jumped out of the saddle. Victorian horsewomen, with this extra security added to good hands and natural sympathy for their mounts, often went better across country than the men. Writers and artists make fun of the foxhunter who "sees the object of his admiration disappearing over a hog-backed stile" which he is afraid to jump, or who to escape "the inconvenience of being beaten by a lady" lands himself in more inconvenience still.

Here a married man who has retired from the splendor of top boots and leather breeches to the inglorious ease of check trousers and carpet slippers helps his wife to mount the hunter that used to be his.

After John Leech in *Ask Mamma*, by R. S. Surtees, 1858

SKIPPER,
the author's horse

In the second half of the nineteenth century riding habits were simplified, for safety as well as neatness. By the nineties a few daring girls, encouraged perhaps by the new vogue for bicycling, actually ventured to ride astride, wearing divided skirts. They were very much frowned upon by traditionalists of both sexes; an Edwardian authoress complained that when a man fell off it proved that he was a dashing horseman, but when a girl fell off it proved that she couldn't ride.

American women seem to have been well in advance of their European contemporaries, and to have set a sensible example which was gradually followed by the rest of the world.

Higher Education from *Punch*, 1880

With the twentieth century has come the successful application of scientific principles to cross-country riding as well as to "academic" equitation. At the same time the fears of the old writers, that "the Amazons" would "add to their spoils, and complete their triumph over us by wearing the breeches," have been realized. Women not merely ride astride but compete with, and often beat, men in all forms of equestrian sport. Perhaps the one thing they may regret in the present state of affairs is that horsewomen now so greatly outnumber horsemen.

Inglorious now the Trojan horsemen yield
Camilla rides in Triumph through the field.

From PENELOPE by Norman Thelwell,
published by Methuen Limited, 1972

Princess Cynisca of Sparta (so Xenophon tells us) won the chariot race at the Olympic Games with a team which she did not drive, or even water herself. Her brother the King had encouraged her to enter so that the Spartans could learn from her example that there was no merit in a sport in which even women could succeed, and so stop wasting money on racehorses. Another better example is set by Princess Anne of Britain, whose participation has done much to encourage the sport of Combined Training. A former Champion of Europe, Princess Anne was a member of the British Olympic Team in 1976.

That brings us full circle (with Xenophon): time has come round and where I did begin there will I end.

Princess Anne and Doublet at Crookham